HIGHER EDUCATION
IN A MATURING DEMOCRACY

HIGHER EDUCATION
IN A MATURING
DEMOCRACY

by Louis G. Geiger

Introduction by Irvin G. Wyllie

UNIVERSITY OF NEBRASKA PRESS
Lincoln   1963

Publishers on the Plains

UNP

Copyright © 1963 by the University of Nebraska Press

All rights reserved

Library of Congress Catalog Card Number 63-20208

Manufactured in the United States of America

First Printing October, 1963
Second Printing September, 1964

Introduction

WHILE STANDING vacant-minded in a cafeteria
line not long ago I had an unexpected encounter that improved my understanding of American education, and my appreciation of its
intimate relation to democracy. A few pleas-
antries volunteered by a stranger at my side
made me aware that he was a foreign visitor,
eager for contact with Americans. I invited him
to join me, not only because the exchange promised to be agreeable, but because he had already,
through his unembarrassed forwardness, paid
the United States the distinct compliment of
adopting its democratic manners and informal
style of social intercourse. My new-found companion proved to be a young biochemist from
Pakistan who, like young Americans of a hundred years ago who went abroad to attend German universities, had come to America for
advanced training. His American mentor was a

[v]

scientist of international repute who had taken a position at a small midwestern university when it appeared that he might be cut off from his highest aspirations by the closed and rigid academic system of his native Sweden. At the time of our encounter my young friend was visiting Madison, Wisconsin, seeking help with his research problem from biochemists at the University of Wisconsin.

In our time together we dwelt only briefly on the Kashmir dispute and the saga of Lyndon Johnson's favorite Pakistani camel driver. What my companion was most eager to talk about was his discovery of the magnitude, variety, and general excellence of the American educational system. "Before coming here," he said, "I knew that America educated her masses, but I could not imagine that institutions created for the masses could also train scholars of the highest quality." He went on to say that the unity of the American system was one of its great strengths. "A comprehensive but unified system identifies talent of all kinds and brings it to the top, and through the free internal circulation of new knowledge provides the means for constant improvement all along the line." I volunteered that critics often equated American mass education with mediocrity. "That opinion may have some basis in fact," he replied, "but it fails to account for the brilliant men you produce, and in relation to the ordinary man it ignores the comparative view. Even where you get only a mediocre product you must remember that many nations get no product at all, because they fail to educate their masses. I have not seen in America, as I have in other countries, an illiterate peasantry or a hopelessly ignorant working class."

My young friend's decision to come to the United States had been shaped by an experience at an international scientific congress in Moscow a few years ago. Of the papers delivered at that gathering, he reported, sixty per cent were read by Americans; and of the American papers, eighty per cent were by men still in their twenties and early thirties. "The extreme youth of the Americans stunned the other delegations. Time after time a senior scientist from France, Germany, Sweden or the Soviet Union shared the program with two Americans who were his juniors by thirty or forty years." Since there were no significant qualitative differences among the papers, the age difference was all the more impressive. "How is it possible," the Pakistani asked himself, "for the United States to produce so many able scientists, so young?"

The answer, he decided, must be concealed in some distinctive feature of American education. After several months in the United States he thought he had discovered the secret. "You have more academic freedom here than anywhere else in the world," he declared. By academic freedom he meant unlimited academic opportunity, as well as freedom of teaching and inquiry. In his view the variety and comprehensiveness of American education makes it possible to identify and cultivate many different natural talents, and to provide training consistent with the individual's choice of goal. He observed that those who chose academic goals could be reasonably certain of finding posts in America's ever-expanding educational establishment, and of climbing up the ladder as fast and as far as their performance would allow. "In America," said the Pakistani, "the young man does not have to wait for his professorship until an old man dies. In every line and every department there are many professors, not just one. And young men are free to determine the direction of their own work. The situation is quite different elsewhere, where old professors, through their monopoly of power, control and sometimes destroy the careers of younger men. The American system encourages originality and ambition in the young."

Though my companion undoubtedly underestimated the extent to which the evils of which he spoke also operate in the United States, he was quite right in his general assessment of the comparative openness of the American educational establishment, and of its reflection of the democratic values of the society of which it is a part. Beyond that he understood, as many American critics have not, that mass education provides the best possible foundation for excellence at the highest levels.

At the time of our chance meeting I had not expected to be instructed on American education by a foreign guest, but I was. Readers of the essays that follow have more reason to expect to be instructed by Professor Louis Geiger of Colorado College, who has made substantial scholarly contributions to the history of American higher education, and is especially expert on the land-grant institutions that dominate the intellectual life of the Great Plains. Like my friend from Pakistan, he has had an opportunity to observe education in other parts of the world, and can therefore deliver informed and sometimes devastating comparative judgments. "It is the professors," he writes, "who are chiefly responsible for the fact that the society of Western Kansas compares favorably in general sophistication, worldliness, and manners with that of rural France." At the same time, his comparative knowledge permits him to criticize our education for failing to make American women as economically productive as the women of Finland and the Soviet Union. Throughout, Professor Geiger's central concern is the complex role of higher education in a democracy.

What is most refreshing in these essays is the author's independence of mind, his refusal to settle for conventional wisdom, his abhorrence of clichés and intellectual stereotypes. He knows it is fashionable to deplore American departures from educational tradition, but he refuses to be fashionable, insisting that defenders of traditional education plainly do not know "what a failure it really was, both in content and quality." Yet he is not given to glossing over the shabbiness and anti-intellectual character of many contemporary educational practices. He faces facts for what they are, and boldly calls them by their names.

Because he is impatient with conventional interpretations, Professor Geiger is able to see new significance in familiar arrangements.

Everyone knows that land-grant colleges offered military training to their students. But who has stopped to think that this arrangement helped to civilianize the armed forces of the United States, prevent the development of a European military caste in our midst, and make the generals and admirals, in some respects at least, the subordinates of professors and laboratory scientists? Professor Geiger has equally fresh observations to make concerning higher education's contribution to the settlement of the West, the growth of the economy, the conservation of human resources, the improvement of public discourse and public service, and the elevation of the cultural level of the United States. Though prepared originally for audiences of academic deans and colleagues, these essays can be appreciated by anyone willing to re-examine his own ideas about education in a democracy.

IRVIN G. WYLLIE
Department of History
University of Wisconsin

Contents

THE EDUCATIONAL REVOLUTION
AND AMERICAN DEMOCRACY

The Educational Revolution and American Democracy

MY INTENTION is not to attempt a general critique of education in America, but rather to limit the discussion to some remarks upon the relation of a hundred-year revolution in higher education, one that is still in progress, to the development of the ideals and practices of democracy in America. I am aware that our system of education has been no perfect instrument, that it is guilty of errors and failures, that it has even created major problems. But it is also important to point out that Americans are still convinced that, failures and all, its benefits for them far outweigh its deficiencies.

The starting point of any discussion of higher education and democracy in America must obviously be the Morrill Land-Grant College Act, which was signed by President Lincoln on July

2, 1862. The act was almost unnoticed in the news of the day. Only the day before, McClellan had been thrown back in the last of the grinding Seven Days' Battles before Richmond. Shiloh had been fought only a few months earlier, Antietam was two months in the future. This was also the year of the Emancipation Proclamation and the Homestead Act. Yet there have been far more celebrations of the Morrill Act centennial than of the events which claimed public attention a century ago. It was the general theme of the 1961 annual meeting of the Association of American Universities and Land-Grant Colleges, and public colleges all over the nation have celebrated it. A task force report of the Hoover Commission in 1949 described the act as the "most effective grant-in-aid ever made by the Federal Government," and in 1953 the National Manpower Council called it the "most important single governmental step in connection with the training of scientific and professional personnel."[1]

The revolutionary effects of the colleges

[4]

launched under the Morrill Act were the admission of a host of new subjects to the precincts of higher education and the demonstration that higher education for the masses was workable. These innovations have proved hardly less important for private colleges than for the public ones. All American higher education has been revolutionized by them. All aspects of American life have been affected. Since 1862, every profession has come to be based on college training, and caste-tainted apprenticeship has nearly disappeared. Our educational revolution of the last century has had effects far beyond our frontiers. From isolated backwaters, American campuses have developed into international communities. Such educational outposts as Montana State College attract streams of pilgrims from Africa and Asia, and their faculties roam the world from Ethiopia, to Iran, to the Philippines. Leaders of underdeveloped countries have come to recognize the ignorance of their masses as their greatest deficiency. And since World War II, the idea of higher education for the masses, largely ignored in Europe except in Russia, has caught on in such strongholds of elitism as England and Germany.

The revolution in higher education actually began long before 1862. What the Morrill Act did was to mark a victory for the advocates of a thorough reform of American colleges. In his last years George Washington planned for a national university in the new capital, and Thomas Jefferson's last project was the organization of the University of Virginia, a unique institution designed to enlist higher education in the service of democracy. Jefferson, and Washington too, anticipated the view expressed by a member of the California Board of Regents in 1872 when he said that the "state is bound to furnish the citizen the means of discharging the duties it imposes on him; if the state imposes duties that require intelligence, it is the office of the state to furnish the means of intelligence."[2]

The great surge of educational reformism that developed in the mid-nineteenth century was part of freedom's ferment, a reflection of the experimental and reforming energies of the Jackson era. With the achievement of universal white male suffrage and office holding, an elementary education for everyone became imperative. Jacksonian democracy had conferred power on the masses but not necessarily restraint and judgment, and it had raised their aspirations without providing the machinery to satisfy them. It is significant that the 1840's and 1850's were a turbulent time in which democracy often skirted close to mobocracy. The democratic-Enlightenment doctrine of man's improvability added conviction to reformers' efforts. By 1860 Americans had accepted the principle of free, tax-supported, nonsectarian elementary education, and they had taken the first steps toward replacing the ne'er-do-well schoolmaster who "kept" school with the normal-trained school-marm who "taught."

Less immediately effective and less noticeable because it touched fewer people was the simultaneous movement to reform the old American colleges and their curricula, little changed since colonial times. Some of the colleges' own graduates were their most outspoken critics, among them Daniel Coit Gilman, Henry Tappan, Andrew D. White, and Francis Wayland. Most of them also knew first hand the vigorous new German universities that had grown out of an early nineteenth-century cultural revival. From them the American reformers had learned about scholarship, research, and academic freedom. These now familiar concepts were hardly even understood—much less practiced—in American institutions. Branding American colleges as intellectual backwaters offering neither cultural nor useful training, their critics attacked in particular the devotion to dry-as-dust classics, gerund-grinding, and the preoccupation with minor details of student behavior.

Some of the modern critics of American higher education, including David Riesman, imply that the masses have pulled down our colleges from an eminence of learning they once occupied. The historical facts are otherwise. Louis Agassiz described Harvard in 1850 as a "respectable high school where they taught the dregs of learning."[3] In 1867, James A. Garfield, a Williams graduate, said that he had examined the catalogs of some twenty colleges and found them all alike. To earn a bachelor's degree at Harvard, which was better than most, a student devoted four-sevenths of a four-year course to "the history, oratory, and poetry of Greece and Rome." He found no mention of "physical geography, of anatomy, physiology, or the general history of the United States. A few weeks of the senior year given to Guizot, the history of the Federal Constitution, and a lecture on general history once a week during half a year, furnish all that a graduate of Harvard is required to know of his own country and the living nations of the earth . . . ." Garfield had not found English literature in any of the curricula he examined.[4] Charles Eliot, who would reform Harvard shortly after Garfield spoke, wrote in his reminiscences that in 1870 when he proposed to the Harvard Medical School that written examinations replace five-minute oral quizzes he was told that "Written examinations are impossible for the Medical School. A majority of the students cannot write well enough."[5]

Another current of higher educational reform sprang from the great scientific advances that were being made in the laboratories of European universities. Still another example for Americans was the practical, yet rigorous, German technical high school of agriculture and mechanics. Most of whatever applied research Americans undertook they carried on outside the colleges, where courses in science and technology were unsystematic and elementary. As late as 1850 not a single college had a laboratory, and the typical library, in the words of one college president, consisted of "old theology books and other lumber . . . opened once a week by the professor of Latin and Greek and kept open for half an hour."[6]

However, the first steps toward bringing science and technology into the colleges had been taken before the Civil War in such institutions as West Point (1802), Rensselaer (1824), and

[10]

the Sheffield and Lawrence Scientific Schools of Yale and Harvard. In the late 1850's the states of Pennsylvania, Michigan, and Iowa opened state-supported agricultural schools, without, however, settling the question of whether they should be colleges or high schools. By 1862 there were about twenty institutions in this country of thirty million people that could be classed as scientific. But even in these, science was taught for its own sake, treated somewhat like litera-ture, a subject to be studied but not used.[7]

The new ideas on education coincided with growing evidence that even the limited public which had access to the colleges was losing con-fidence in them. On the eve of the Civil War, college enrollments were not keeping up with the rise in population. The champions of the "industrial classes" declared that the colleges were unsuited to their needs, and indifferent to them, and that elementary education was not enough. Jonathan Baldwin Turner, a Yale grad-uate teaching at Illinois College (a sectarian institution), usually receives the credit for the

idea of using the vast reserve of the public do-
main to endow agricultural and mechanical colleges. The fact that the public lands had been
used since the late eighteenth century to support
public schools and private colleges, as well as
the infant state universities of the upper middle
west, and that they were being used in the
1850's to subsidize private rail and canal com-
panies, gave precedent to this form of support.
It is worth remarking that only one day after
President Lincoln signed the college bill, he
signed the bill underwriting the Union Pacific
railroad with a great land grant.

The mixed influences and purposes pulling
and hauling at the American people as they established their first system of higher education
were to give it a peculiarly American form—a
combination of the German university, the German technical high school, and the American
college. The two American contributions to
this structure were by design in the one case
and partly accidental in the other. The first
was the conception of mass higher education,

generated by reformers. The second American contribution was the structure itself, which grew out of the simple fact that the American college was too well established to be eliminated by the revolutionaries; they had to build on it. This has meant that preprofessional general education has been retained at the collegiate level. The close association of general education with professional specialization has been responsible for improved scholarship in undergraduate education, and a broader outlook in professional schools and their graduates than they might have if they were isolated. The classical-humanist studies benefited almost as much as the new professional-technological curricula from the idea, new to American colleges, that knowledge was a growing, living thing, and that professors were expected to contribute to it as well as to pass it on. Moreover, the general education subjects were placed at an age level where they could be fully appreciated.

It is unlikely that the Morrill supporters foresaw all these long-term benefits, but they definitely supported the combined curriculum. Although the Morrill Act required that the new "people's colleges" have as their principal object the teaching of "agriculture and the mechanic arts," it added that "other scientific and classical subjects should not be excluded." The grand objective of the act was defined as "the liberal and practical education of the industrial classes in the several pursuits and professions of life."[8] Jonathan Turner saw the colleges as the source of a liberal education for the ninety-nine per cent of the population whose occupations were not based on higher education. Senator Morrill, who had never gone to college, agreed with these aims but added that his measure "was designed to largely benefit those at the bottom of the ladder who wanted to climb up . . . ."[9]

The relationship of the cultural and the practical is deeply embedded in American thinking about higher education. In 1961 Whitney J. Oates, Director of the Council of the Humanities at Princeton, declared without challenge at the centennial convention of the Land-

Grant Colleges and State Universities that it was an "incontestable doctrine" that the best balanced institutions (by which he meant those equally strong in the humanities and the sciences) were in fact the *best* institutions for training specialists as well as anyone else. In the past generation there has been far more concern about the role, the quality, and the content of general education in our colleges than there has been about professional training. Americans are reasonably satisfied with the quality of the latter offered by their universities. Few of the thousands of our students who go abroad nowadays do so to get the best professional training available in their chosen fields, as they had to do in the nineteenth century. It is general education that they now seek, in some not-too-certain combination of learning a language and "soaking up atmosphere."

The American university as we know it had developed by 1900. Also by that time a mixture of institutional types—the private college, the sectarian college, and the private, public, and sectarian universities—had been organized into a kind of national system. This had been achieved by such self-policing and standardizing agencies as the Association of American Universities and the Association of Land-Grant Colleges. A national academic currency, the credit-hour, was an essential invention. With its general acceptance, the American student could migrate from coast to coast, from private college, to sectarian, to public, and back again. Scores of new professional societies[10] drew academicians together for scholarly discourse, to prescribe courses of study, and to set standards of excellence. The professional self-consciousness of the new breed of college teacher, manifested in the founding of the American Association of University Professors in 1915, contributed also to the unity of the new educational establishment.

None of this could have occurred had there not been a simultaneous rise of public interest. Horatio Alger's tales of young men rising in the world illustrates the utilitarian and anti-intellectual climate of the Gilded Age, a climate that had been conditioned if not caused by the old colleges' loss of prestige. The villain of these simple pieces is often a fellow who has been to college. He speaks affectedly and is generally offensive. He has learned to connive but not to work. Eventually he is thoroughly discomfited by the poor and hard-working lad who has not been ruined by too much education. But from this distrust of what seemed snobbish and useless, Americans moved to an almost religious faith in higher education. The most recent evidence of such faith is the rapidly rising number of adults taking college courses offering no credit.[11]

The Morrill Act and the Land Act of 1881[12] were intended to prime the pump of local support, and they were largely the work of reformers, not the result of spontaneous public demand. Baited by the offer of land grants, states and territories lost little time in getting colleges started, only to learn that the new institutions cost far more than the federal endowment produced. By the end of the century the

states' contribution had become the major support of public higher education, and so it has
remained. Meantime, old institutions under-
went a thorough overhauling. Philanthropists
entered the field in force to support them or to
found new colleges. A demand for an educated
clergy and fears of the consequences of godless
education stimulated the churches to renewed
vigor in a field they had once largely dominated.

A brand-new missionary spirit that pervaded
the new and revived colleges played no small
part in convincing the public that the new education and the accompanying research were useful, and in convincing the "plowboys and greasy
mechanics" (as elitists called them) that higher
education was indeed possible for the likes of
them. The colleges were obviously and eagerly
useful in training teachers, lawyers, and engi-
neers, all in short supply, particularly in newly
settled regions. Experiment stations and laboratories set out to explore a region's potential,
and attacked such local problems as a cure for
wheat stem rust or the proper construction of

privies. Extension programs and correspondence courses, both developed after the Civil War, literally took the colleges to the people who could not come to them. Intercollegiate athletics, especially football, won over a segment of the population that was not likely to be impressed by the installation of a chapter of Phi Beta Kappa. The point is that the new institutions, private or public, and likewise the proud old ones, were learning to be colleges of democracy. And Americans were learning, somewhat reluctantly, to accept the laboratory, the library, and the cultivated human mind as the only reliable sources of whatever truths or revelations would be vouchsafed to mankind.

The movement to make higher education immediately useful in the vocational and professional sense reached its peak in the period between 1900 and 1930. Useful courses of study —or so they were labeled—and specialized academic degrees for those who completed them proliferated in a truly wonderful way. The few who rose to question the materialistic emphasis were ignored. The most hopeful development of the times—but a disquieting one too because of the barrenness of many collegiate offerings—was the considerable increase of college enrollments after World War I. The reformers' dream of mass higher education had been accepted by the masses themselves. The sharp climb in enrollments which began in the 1920's has been interrupted only temporarily by the extraordinary circumstances of the Great Depression and World War II.

For a generation now we have been in the third and perhaps the final stage of this particular educational revolution. This has been distinguished by the effort to reconcile popularity with quality, and to complete the synthesis of the newer utilitarian with the older cultural and moral purposes of our higher education.

In this hasty sketch of the history of the educational revolution, I have already indicated some of its contributions to democracy. Let me turn now to a more specific treatment, noting first of all that the revolution occurred while the republic was being subjected to one strain after the other. The Civil War, during which the Morrill Act was passed, was followed by the scarcely less painful experience of reunification, which was not really completed until nearly a generation after Reconstruction was officially over. Simultaneously the rural, agricultural, and pioneering country that Jackson and Lincoln knew, became in the short space of a few decades the great urban society and industrial producer it is today. The boom was slowed by periodic busts, each resulting in shaken confidence in democracy. A flood of immigrants, alien in culture and religion, poured into the nation. Boodlers and robber barons laughed at the law and common decency. The mild class tensions of a happier day hardened into class hatreds. Industrial employers and their employees lived in a state of armed conflict, and the northern workingmen's slum joined the Negro freedmen's shacks as a part of the American scene.

In the twentieth century two world wars and

the wearisome Cold War brought an unprece-
dented expansion of the military establishment.
Great states and small, old and young, collapsed
on every side. Yet the American republic weath-
ered every crisis, domestic and foreign, military,
and ideological. It not only survived, but undertook the physical and moral reconstruction of
half the world. In the great crises of the 1940's
and 1950's no other nation came anywhere near
being able to muster the great strength, the
imagination, the good sense and good will, the
restraint and judgment, that the task required.
This was a demonstration of maturity that even
Americans had not known they possessed. No
institutions had done so much to bring it about
as the universities born in the educational
revolution.

One of the most significant contributions
of the educational revolution to a continued
healthy democracy, indeed to its revival in the
era of Gilded Age cynicism, was to provide the
means to satisfy the soaring aspirations of the
multitude. Writing in the 1830's, Alexis de

Tocqueville had thought that one of democracy's greatest dangers lay in its encouraging the masses at the bottom of the ladder to aspire to a top that was out of their reach. When agricultural science and engineering were raised from vocations to professions by way of collegiate preparatory programs, the way was opened to an almost unlimited expansion of opportunities for professional status. In short, the educational revolution gave substance to, and even enlarged the possibilities of, the self-made tradition. Bootstrap opportunities, once almost entirely limited to the business world, to farming, or to lucky strikes in mining, were extended to the sciences, government service (including opportunities in striped-pants diplomacy for descendants of slaves, e.g., Ralph Bunche), to the arts, and to a steadily enlarging list of professions. To put it more graphically, higher education was a device for the conservation of human resources that had been hitherto wasted.

And in the process our society became "freer, more adaptable, more kinetic" than it ever was in the nineteenth century. The farm boy, once limited to following in his father's footsteps or taking the long chance of running away to frontier or city, has found a far more reliable route and a broader range of choice by way of his state university. City colleges have served the same purpose for immigrants' children. President Kennedy's cabinet has at least one member of unpromising origin who arrived where he is by this route, and the two recent appointees to the Supreme Court are self-made men via higher education. The President himself is only two generations removed from the same circumstances. These are only conspicuous examples of a mass social mobility engineered by the new universities.

The movement to suburbia and the sharp decline in farm population in the past half-century have owed far more to the colleges and universities than to the urgings of government agencies or the blandishments of Chambers of Commerce—people do not change jobs because a bureaucrat or salesman says they should. Indeed, it has not been until comparatively recently that we have begun to recognize at all the necessity of shifting people out of agriculture, and stopped the search—an old favorite with publicists—for ways to keep our farm-bred youngsters at home. Actually, almost from their origin even the most avowedly agricultural and mechanical colleges, founded to make farmers prosperous and happy rather than to get them out of the business altogether, were doing the latter, more or less unconsciously. Their engineering branches developed ahead of the agricultural ones and attracted the boys "too smart to farm," as the farmers themselves put it. Some state colleges, dependent upon locally oriented legislatures for funds, are still half-afraid to admit they are preparing their students for a national, not a local, occupational market. Farm to city migration has assumed the proportions of a folk movement; as significant as its magnitude, however, has been the fact that no great social unrest has accompanied it. In the past fifty years there have been no peasant uprisings, not even a revival of the People's Party. Physical and occupational mobility have been a major contributor to Americans' stability and contentment.

Higher education has also aided social stability by its contribution to the continued material abundance which has been a characteristic of the American experience from the days of colonization. Economic plenty is no guarantee of democracy, but it unquestionably is a help. An abundance of goods has undermined tendencies to develop privileged status in this country, and contributed to the openhandedness associated with Americans. Underdeveloped countries seem to have particular difficulty in finding the selflessness or the public spirit, the concern for all instead of oneself, the easy social relationships that are characteristic of our well-fed working democracy.

Almost to the end of the nineteenth century our agricultural abundance was largely a result of fertile land. But the great plenty of food and fiber we had would undoubtedly be wanting by now, were it not for the work of the agricultural colleges and their allied experiment stations. In industry, by 1900 we created an economic miracle out of a combination of a national habit of work, hard-driving entrepreneurs, low-paid labor from the farm and from Europe, and resources of coal and iron. But with no more than these, Nikita Khrushchev's well-advertised burial project might already be completed. Toward the end of the century the college-trained engineer assumed increasing importance in economic development, and the colleges' role was further expanded before World War I with the development of such pioneering institutions as the Mellon Institute of Industrial Research. Now no industrial producer worth an investor's notice is without a research staff—all trained by the universities. (There were three hundred industrial laboratories in 1921, and five thousand in 1956.)[13] We have arrived at the day when we no longer depend upon the stray genius for industrial or scientific advances. Instead, a host of comparatively ordinary men and women, trained, organized, and equipped, have not only relieved us of the necessity of waiting for an Edison or the Wright brothers to show up, but have outdone them in ideas and inventiveness as well.

The role of education—that is, investment in human resources—in economic growth has not been thoroughly explored by scholars of economics, but Theodore Schultz, in his presidential address before the American Economic Association in 1960, suggested that as much as three-fifths and no less than one-third of the rise in our national income between 1929 and 1956 was owing to investment in the training of human beings. He declared that "the most distinctive feature of our economic growth is the growth in human capital. Without it there would be only hard, manual work and poverty except for those who have income from property." (This is a description of landed aristocracy.) Without training, most of us would be, he said, quoting William Faulkner, men " 'without skills and knowledge leaning terrifically against nothing.' " Speaking of the backward countries, Schultz observed that it was "simply . . . not possible [for them] to have the fruits of a modern agriculture and the abundance of modern industry without making large investments in human beings."[14]

In the realm of government we are depending more and more upon the expert, the educated man. Indeed, our whole conduct of public affairs, our expectations of our public officials, even the tone of our public discourse have undergone more improvement than most of us realize in the past two generations. Public debate has assumed a decorum all too rare a century ago when the smear, not even recognized as such, was the common currency of politics. It seems more than coincidence that early in this century Theodore Roosevelt and Woodrow Wilson, both graduates of universities in the forefront of the educational revolution, introduced an enlarged concept of responsibility and informed leadership to the office of the Presidency. With one or possibly two exceptions, their successors have looked to them as models and not to their outmoded, sometimes tarnished predecessors of the post-Civil War era.

Since Roosevelt, Wilson, and La Follette, the American voters, themselves no longer men with the bark on, have turned increasingly to college and professionally trained men to handle their public business. In cosmopolitan outlook and in their conceptions of public responsibility our representatives are generally an improvement over their predecessors of a century ago.

One can emphasize the point of the effect of the new higher education upon the public services of the American democracy in no better way than by noting its effects upon the military branches and upon our conduct of foreign affairs. The replacement of the cavalry boot and breeches by slacks and low shoes in World War II was as symbolic of a changing spirit in the military as of the end of the cavalry itself. It was the German missile experts that we and the Russians brought home after the war, not the German generals. And presently the men of

Canaveral, all trained at universities, are over-shadowing the men from the service academies. Although we have not yet quite acknowledged this to ourselves, it seems clear that in 1962 Americans—and Russians too—are shifting an increasing amount of responsibility for national defense to universities and laboratories. Advanced academic degrees are replacing blood and guts in the services themselves, and since World War II the academies have been relying increasingly upon the universities for educational models and the training of their faculties. The civilian and military are being drawn together into the common mold of American democracy.[15]

In the field of foreign relations we have undertaken a revision of policy and a reversal of firmly held public convictions that might well have been impossible without the aid of higher education for the masses. A half-century or so ago only Theodore Roosevelt and a few other young mavericks and academicians had any understanding that the times required a departure from our traditional policy of isolation. In a little more than a generation after T. R., no time at all in the long sweep of history, the newest of the world powers took the lead in forming a new international system based on cooperation. Americans had moved at a tremendous pace from a policy of isolation—which had served them well for a century—to world involvement. The enlarged understanding and broadened outlook necessary to this change were at least partially the result of informed and objective teaching of history and the social sciences in the new colleges. The term "social science" itself indicates the new approach to the study of human problems. By the 1940's several generations of Americans had acquired a reasonably sound understanding of their own country and the world, and of human behavior as well. Even more directly the colleges had done much to arouse and inform the public by making themselves open forums for the discussion of public issues.

The truly astonishing result in our own time

is not the foot-dragging, the grumbling about international giveaways, or the impatient demands that we have it out with the Russians and get it over with. It is that the one thing upon which our two major parties are more or less agreed is continued active participation in world affairs. It is hard to imagine the Americans of 1898, who so hotheadedly rushed into a needless war with Spain, having the patience and cool judgment required to fight an inconclusive and limited war in Korea, to endure the long strain of the Cold War, or not to smash Castro.

The colleges and universities of the educational revolution have been an essentially conservative force in our public life, that is, conservative in relation to the forces for change that surrounded them. The early sponsors of the new higher education were almost all conservatives in any current use of the term, and they expected general dissemination of learning to be a force for stability. William Blackburn, a Presbyterian minister and state university president, could have been speaking for all of them when he told a visiting legislative committee in 1884 that it was the university's function to bring law and order to an era distinguished by a "wild hatred of wealth." "We must educate the young men of today," he said, "so that they will not become the mad socialists of tomorrow."[16] Subsequent events have borne out this expectation, although not always in the way Blackburn and his fellows probably expected. The new colleges did not make many socialists or even change many Republicans to Democrats, but they did subject "the American past, present and future" to a "critical scrutiny that helped to shape a social awareness and a social outlook" which has become the basis for a general "unconscious progressivism."[17] The continuation of the evolutionary pace that was fixed in our tradition and style by the Founding Fathers owes much to the moderate progressive temper fostered by the educational revolution. The same may be said for the successful adaptation of the democracy associated with Jefferson and

Jackson to an urban, industrial world, and now a militarized one. The conservative reformers of the turbulent 1870's and 1880's would be pleased to note that there has been far less talk of imminent social revolution, and less ground for it, in the twentieth century than there was in their day.

The educational revolution also helped to elevate the culture of a rough-hewn democracy and to preserve the morals of a society being torn from its traditions. Owing to their unique combination of the liberal arts college with the graduate and professional schools, American institutions of higher education have always been concerned with the broad spectrum of the arts in general. Early in the revolution they opened their halls to visiting artists or to art scholars. Extension programs often attempted to rival the old lyceums in breadth of offering. In the early years of this century the Universities of Wisconsin, Minnesota, and North Dakota were separately and jointly sponsoring tours of performing artists, sometimes professionals and sometimes faculty members themselves.

In due time, tiny departments of fine arts, often beginning as adjuncts to the teacher-training program, developed into university colleges and schools, while instruction in performance and appreciation made its way into the traditional liberal arts curriculum. In our time colleges have become centers of creativity as well as schools of instruction. Wagnerian opera at the University of Indiana, a multi-million dollar fine arts center at the University of Missouri, a vigorous creative writing program at the University of Iowa, rare book collections at the University of Texas, a week-long symposium at Colorado College on "The Contemporary Arts and the Citizen," these are only a few examples of a general phenomenon on the American campus. In the course of this notable development educational institutions have assumed the role of art patrons. The painter, writer, or composer in residence is now a commonplace at the American college. Milton Babbitt, Chairman of the Department of Music at Princeton, has said that the development and patronage of musical composition on the campus is a "purely contemporary and American phenomenon."[18]

I am not prepared to say just how, or how much, these efforts have enriched our mass culture, but there is hardly any doubt that the effect has been significant. There has been a thorough filtration from the colleges to the masses, not only through the increasingly large segment of our people attending the colleges themselves, but by way of the public schools. Professor Peter Munch, an Oslo-trained sociologist now teaching at Southern Illinois University, has observed that the aspect of American public schools which impressed him most when he first came to the United States was the large role allotted to performance and appreciation of the fine arts.

We have already indicated some effects of education upon the moral conduct of our citizens. In the larger sense the propagation of the ideals of scholarship and research has effected improvements in, and tempered the conduct of, our entire society and its institutions. The even tone of contemporary religious debate owes much to the fact that an educated clergy and their equally educated parishioners are less willing now than formerly to damn as infidels or heretics all those who differ with them. In Lincoln's time, when Baptists and Methodists considered education dangerous to religious faith, sectarian strife was the order of the day, and mob action was not an infrequent accompaniment of religious difference. Catholics have modified the narrow views and aggressive behavior that so alarmed Protestants in the 1850's, and it has been a good while since the Protestants have burned a convent or surreptitiously passed around *The Awful Disclosures of Maria Monk*. At the same time, the active social concern of all religious groups has grown as their orthodoxy has been tempered and their educational level raised.

Even the social climbing to professional status

—that is, to equality at the top—which was encouraged by the educational revolution has had its effect on our morals. The much coveted professional badge has implied not only collegiate training but a high standard of behavior as well. The ethical codes of organized occupations are not cynical devices to deceive the public, although crooks still can and do operate happily under them. I have never heard of, say, the formal rules of conduct subscribed to by land speculators of the 1840's and 1850's. In their day it was almost the accepted practice for a congressman to speculate in the public lands. In one instance at least, a substantial family fortune was founded by several brothers using advance information they gained in Congress to beat the general public to low-priced but enormously valuable pine lands. They were never touched by even the breath of scandal. Billie Sol Estes would hardly have been considered dishonest in the 1870's. More likely, he would have founded a great American fortune and endowed a university in Pecos. The contrast between the response of W. K. Vanderbilt when confronted with his public responsibilities in the 1880's and Roger Blough in a somewhat similar situation in 1962 is not without meaning. The former's was simply "The public be damned." Blough carefully and patiently explained to another, and undamned, public why he thought it necessary to raise the price of steel, and then bowed to the public's representative, the President of the United States.

What could be a more important contribution to the moral standard of an entire society than the establishment of ability, or individual human worth, as the measure of human beings instead of race, religion, ancestry, or social position? A brief excursion to any newspaper of no more than fifty years ago will illustrate my point. The unashamed snobbery of the small-town press of the 1880's is something of a shock in the 1960's. Prejudices were freely displayed with little thought or concern that they would offend anyone who mattered. This was hardly surprising when even Columbia University

professors were teaching that Anglo-Saxon su-
periority was a demonstrable fact.[19] Thomas
Jefferson and the Jacksonian reformers had
launched the first attacks on the old tests, but it
was not until the educational revolution had
affected a large part of American society that
they were really discredited. The new social and
biological sciences exposed them for the frauds
they were, and the new colleges and universities
made this information the common property of
the educated masses.

The revival of the struggle for full rights for
the Negro waited upon the broad dissemination
of higher education among both whites and
Negroes—upon the sharpened sense of social jus-
tice it brought to the one and the self-respect
and skill it gave the other. The sad example of
the University of Mississippi notwithstanding,
integration has moved faster in southern institutions of higher education and with fewer diffi-
culties than it has in churches, public schools,
or in rest-rooms. In April, 1962, an Associated
Press dispatch reported that in a poll of the stu-

dents of a half-dozen southern colleges from South Caorlina to Texas integration was voted down only once, and then by no overwhelming margin.[20] It was not the students of Tulane University who stood outside a New Orleans school and shrieked obscenities at terrified Negro children whose only offense was that they wanted to enter the wide-open competition of ability.

The seemingly endless testing of abilities and aptitudes that we must undergo these days, and the professional testers with their calculating machines and their calculating minds are symbols of a refinement of democracy. The moral effect of the "institutionalization of reason," as Clinton Rossiter has called it, has been at least as important in making us a better people as the pre-Civil War colleges' emphasis on direct moral instruction. This is no more than the fathers of the revolution expected, although they were likewise convinced that direct instruction in morality-citizenship must not be neglected.

The comparatively disinterested and free intellectual experience of campus life, where the special pleader must submit his case to the tests of reason and truth, is also the most effective schooling in democracy that our society affords. The right to teach and study freely is an extension of the right of free speech, and it is a matter of deep significance for democracy that the degree to which the ideals of academic freedom are observed has become a major test of quality for our colleges and universities. Residence in the comparatively uninhibited free market of ideas that our campuses represent, the opportunity to think, write, and speak with "no restrictions whatsoever," is an unforgettable experience, as important perhaps as the formal training that our colleges provide. Hardly less impressive is the corollary concern with integrity and performance, the emphasis upon *what* one does rather than on *who* one is or what one has. Of all our educational institutions none is less subject to influences of family or connections than our colleges, rich or poor, public or private. It was different once. When Theodore Roosevelt was at Harvard in the 1880's there was no conscious snobbery in his report to his parents that he ranked well academically among the "gentlemen" in his class.

For a great many of us our college years were our first really free intellectual experience, for it is a sad fact that academic freedom has had difficult going in the public schools. The federal government and the great foundations, contrary to popular fears, have seldom been given to petty searches for offensive doctrines or insistence upon the teaching of some ideological line. Even state legislatures and private college boards have been far less guilty of this sort of harassment than the local groups or individuals who find it all too easy to attack the schools in their neighborhood.

Perhaps the most vital effect of our grand experiment in mass higher education is its becoming the most vivid, the most effective common experience shared by the largest single group of Americans. Some seven million young men and women, nearly half the 18 to 21 age group, will be in American college classrooms in 1970. The percentage will unquestionably increase with each following decade for some time to come. Where the college population will stabilize, no one knows. A shared tradition is essential to the sense of oneness that welds a mass of human beings into a nation. Until the end of the last century the rural-pioneer tradition—from actual or vicarious experience—was the source of the Americans' sense of brotherhood, the common element which more than any other welded uprooted Europeans and Africans into "this American, this new man." Crevecoeur recognized the role of the frontier in the eighteenth century; in the nineteenth century such leaders as Jackson and Lincoln were its living symbols with which Americans—old stock or immigrant—identified themselves. But the frontier is no longer a viable tradition; it is little more than a pleasant folk memory, a hunting ground for television writers, in the world of megalopolis, superhighways, missiles, and jets. The inapplicability of the old tradition, with nothing to replace it, was the cause of much floundering in the half-century after Frederick Jackson Turner celebrated the frontier's disappearance by eloquently reminding us of the role it had played in making us what we were.

In its early stages the educational revolution was something of a divisive force itself. It created a large minority of educated people who had little in common with the uneducated mass, and it fostered a specialization of knowledge which threatened communication between even those who were educated. We were, and still are, faced with the problem of becoming separated from each other in our private cubicles of knowledge. The very mobility and personal opulence of our society, likewise furthered by the educational revolution, has contributed to the elevation of self above community.

For a time it was expected that universal public education in elemenatry and high schools might provide the common experience needed to draw us back together. This expectation did not materialize. Our schools do not speak with a common voice, owing to parochial divisions

[46]

and excessively local orientation and influence. Moreover, our stay in them comes at too young an age for them to be the effective universalizing experience with truth and knowledge that our society requires. (Winston Churchill has testified that even one of the great English public schools failed to awaken him intellectually, that he became interested in learning only after he was well into his twenties.) And church and family are no longer adequate as the bearers of a universal tradition capable of binding together our highly complex society.

For better or worse higher education and its accompanying experience of college living is now the most important single force available for creating a new American style, a national consensus of manners and morals, to replace the frontier, rural consensus that served us so long and so well. The general education of the liberal arts college, the different yet shared experience of professional and graduate training, the extended sojourn in a community of scholars with common standards of excellence and conduct, are becoming the unifying force for a body of Americans that is increasing by the year. It is this experience and the ideals it nourishes that alumni share with professors, parents with children, clergymen with laymen, employers with employees, conservatives with liberals, and specialists with specialists.

Ultimately the experience of higher education, which has transcended provincialism, may also transcend nationalism. Our many experiences since the last war with foreign students on our campuses, or our own at universities abroad, provide everyday demonstrations of this point. The ideals of truth, of freedom of thought and expression, are the universals of the true academic community, wherever it is. Committed by their very nature to resist the party line of special pleaders, the universities of the world, on their way to becoming available to the masses of the world, may be the church universal, the agency of the peace of God that man has sought so long. No other institution of the modern world seems to promise so much.

NOTES

1. Russel Thackrey and Jay Richter, "The Land-Grant Colleges and Universities, 1862–1962: An American Institution," *Higher Education* (March, 1959).

2. Frederick Rudolph, *The American College and University* (New York: Knopf, 1962), p. 278.

3. Edward Danforth Eddy, *Colleges for Our Land and Time* (New York: Harper & Row, 1956), p. 3.

4. Allan Nevins, *The State Universities and Democracy* (Urbana: University of Illinois, 1962), p. 5.

5. *Ibid.*, p. 6.

6. Eddy, *Colleges for Our Land and Time*, p. 3.

7. *Ibid.*, p. 10.

8. Thackrey and Richter, "The Land-Grant Colleges and Universities, 1862–1962," p. 3.

9. *Ibid.*, p. 4.

10. There were one hundred and twenty professional societies by 1908. John S. Brubacher and Willis Rudy, *Higher Education in Transition* (New York: Harper & Row, 1958), p. 184.

11. *New York Times,* September 16, 1962.

12. "An Act to grant lands to Dakota, Montana, Arizona, Idaho, and Wyoming for University purposes," *U. S. Statutes at Large,* XXI, 326.

13. "Missouri Assembly on Higher Education" (University of Missouri, April 8–10, 1962).

14. "Investment in Human Capital," *American Economic Review,* LI (January, 1961), 1–6. This theme was developed further some months later with respect to the specific role

of the land-grant colleges by Mary Jean Bowman (University of Chicago). See "The Land-Grant Colleges and Universities in Human Resource Development," *Journal of Economic History*, XXII (December, 1962), 523–546.

15. See the following essay on "The Land-Grant Idea and the Transformation of the American Frontier" for comment on the direct effect of ROTC upon the character of the American military services.

16. Louis G. Geiger, *University of the Northern Plains* (Grand Forks: University of North Dakota Press, 1958), p. 48.

17. Rudolph, *The American College and University*, p. 468.

18. Letter to Fred Sondermann, Colorado College, August, 1962.

19. Alvin Johnson, *Pioneer's Progress* (Lincoln: University of Nebraska Press, 1960), p. 122.

20. Students at Furman (South Carolina), Davidson (North Carolina), Southern Methodist, Rice, and the University of Texas, all approved integration. At Texas, students favored integration, which already was in force, by a vote of 5,000 to 3,000; and their faculty by 512 to 170 (Denver *Post*, April 17, 1962).

THE LAND-GRANT IDEA AND THE TRANSFORMATION OF AMERICAN SOCIETY

The Land-Grant Idea and the Transformation of American Society

THIS IS A COMMENTARY on the limited role assigned to the revolutionary land-grant college movement by American historians and by most other observers of the American scene. I have limited my illustrations to the area of the "last frontier," by which I mean the Great Plains and eastern Rocky Mountain region, roughly the area west of the great bend of the Missouri River, exclusive of the Pacific Coast. I have restricted myself to this region because it is here that the role of the land-grant college has been most marked. Here land-grant or public higher education has enjoyed a near monopoly. Here the virtues and the failings of public higher education stand out most sharply, for they stand alone with no competition or guidance from powerful private or sectarian institutions.

A land-grant college or university is officially designated as such and has rights to land and money grants from the federal government under the two Morrill Acts (1862 and 1890) as well as under several other federal measures. The term "land-grant idea" is broadly serviceable since the entire American system of public higher education, including that part that had evolved before the passage of the first Morrill Act of 1862, owed its origins to land grants. The official land-grant colleges' own association has itself acknowledged the broadened concept in its successive name changes—from the Association of American Agricultural Colleges and Experiment Stations (the original name adopted in 1887) to the American Association of State Universities and Land-Grant Colleges (adopted in 1961).

When the Morrill Act colleges were first launched, they were more or less set apart by their special land-grants and by the requirement that they teach agriculture and mechanic arts, and that they provide military training. The separation was also sharpened in the beginning by the snobbery of the older traditional institutions, and even by that of neighboring institutions hardly older, but possessing the revered title of a "name" college or university and teaching the traditional curriculum. In North Dakota, farm boys attending the raw little university, founded in 1883, were insufferably superior to the farm boys at "Silo Tech," only seven years younger.

The original land-grant proponents' contention that technological and agricultural training should enjoy equality with traditional subjects led to demands for recognition from other fields, among them teacher training. Moreover, since on the last frontier most of the new public colleges received some kind of land grant, they have become increasingly alike through the years, displaying many of the characteristics of business competition and social climbing in the age of the "robber barons"—fierce rivalry, little cooperation, few acknowledged debts, with copying and duplication at every turn. A recent

[55]

instance of the climb to respectability occurred in North Dakota in 1958, when the major issue in the state elections, scarcely one year after the first Sputnik sailed across the heavens, was a legislative proposal to change the name of the Agricultural College to State University. Most of the separate colleges have now achieved the coveted university title. The normal schools have become colleges, and see university status on the horizon—some have already made the grade. What we have achieved is a system of higher education lacking in system. It is a system in its similarity, and in the consensus on the colleges' role, but it is no system in the sense of working together and sharing in a common enterprise. Competition may be the life of trade, and possibly of religion, but in the field of education it has also been the source of frustration and waste.

The hundredth anniversary of the passage of the Morrill Act fell in 1962. What Senator Justin Morrill and Congress did a century ago, in the middle of the Civil War crisis, was of the utmost importance. But how have historians treated the subject of the role of the land-grant idea when considering the general history of the United States? Our high-school textbooks slight the subject almost entirely, as they do that of American education generally. Most college history textbooks do little better, even though they turn aside briefly for a general complimentary remark. Any second-rate politician or robber baron gets more attention than an educational pioneer. Even some social historians are guilty of slighting the land-grant movement. Nelson Blake's *Short History of American Life* mentions the Morrill Act and the land-grant colleges only once in a short paragraph. Everett Dick's *Sod-House Frontier, 1854-1894,* a widely praised book about the states of the last frontier during the era of the educational renaissance, gives two pages in five hundred to higher education. He does not once mention the Morrill Act or the land-grant colleges.

How about the state colleges' own history faculties? In 1960 Robert Athearn of the University of Colorado published *High Country Empire,* a social and political history of the six states of the Upper Missouri River Basin. He mentioned the Morrill Act only once and the land-grant colleges not at all. A *History of South Dakota,* written by a historian who has been a professor and graduate dean at the state university for thirty years, gives very little space to the role of public higher education. In his classic *Populist Revolt,* John D. Hicks, an eminent American historian who spent almost his entire career at three of our greatest land-grant universities, gives no indication that he ever considered the question of whether land-grant colleges, or higher education, may have had anything to do with the development of the most significant agrarian movement in our history.

In October, 1961, at a conference on Western history in Santa Fe, two hundred and fifty historians from all parts of the nation were present, many of them representing land-grant colleges. For two and a half days they read papers on every conceivable subject that might be related to the West: land policy, agriculture, the Army and the Indians, the fur trade, overland trails, minor political figures, and mountain men. Naturally, there were references to the Civil War centennial and to the hundredth birthday of Frederick Jackson Turner, the founder of the cult of western historiography. But nobody mentioned the Morrill Act centennial or land-grant colleges. Not one historian urged his fellows to launch studies of the role of public higher education in shaping the West.

So much for the historians' record of oversight and neglect. What have the colleges contributed to a better appreciation of themselves as a force in the "emergence of modern America"? The answer is little, if anything. Any number of business firms have kept better archives; many public colleges now nearing their hundredth birthday have yet to establish any systematic archival policy. As for any connected account of their past, most land-grant colleges west of the Missouri have published histories of a sort, but even the best of the genre are house histories, the work of a more or less captive historian on the institution's own payroll.

What have been the results of the interest in land-grant college history stirred up by the reminder that 1962 was a significant anniversary? It may have been a sign of arriving maturity that some colleges seized the opportunity to produce their first creditable history. But one also hears of curious situations that developed as many others set about "having their history done." In one case an administration reportedly wanted a history but was unwilling to spend anything on it—faculty members were urged to do the work in their spare time while teaching full schedules. In another, the administration was willing enough, but none of its historians saw enough professional prestige in such a project to be willing to undertake it. In yet another (it is not a land-grant institution, but illustrates my point) an administration prepared for its centennial celebration by assigning a young historian to the monumental task of writing a history of western higher education, but gave him scarcely three years to do it. Another institution found its historian and got its manuscript, but the latter proved insufficiently "optimistic" and so was passed to a committee for improvement. After some consultation another administration decided that its historians might reveal too much that should be forgotten, and so gave the job of writing its history to its public-relations department. Apparently it occurred to no administration that the proper procedure was to open the archives—if records survived—and to let *any* historian have at them.

Historians themselves are strangely apathetic about this—and why, I do not know. They would be outraged if Standard Oil or the Northern Pacific Railroad were equally careless and secretive. There can be no doubt of the low repute in which college histories are held among most professional historians. I have been made to understand on occasion that my own effort in this field, a history of the University of North Dakota, could hardly be considered on the same plane of respectability as a study, for example, of the French grain trade during the Revolution of 1848, or of the pattern of land transfer in a Nebraska county.

Yet institutional histories of the kind described above provide a substantial part of the factual bases of what general historians and the more specialized educational historians have to say about the development and influence of land-grant education in America. Most of these histories are some variation on the rise-from-rags-to-riches theme, and not much more. Their titles—*Beacon on the Prairie, Beacon O'er Plain and Mountain,* and *Lamp in the Desert*—reveal the general tone. In the beginning all is formless and void; then appear the founders, those bearded worthies whose dusty portraits now grace the wall of some unused hall. (Few of these historians ever suggest that the founders' main motive may have been the booming of a town site.) Next comes the opening scene at Frontier A. & M., a dismal event on an isolated windy prairie, or in a stump-strewn clearing in the great woods. Here appear the tiny but dedicated faculty, the handful of earnest students. The early years are invariably hard; the college nearly goes under, but is saved. All ends well, in a steady progress onward and upward, bigger and better, to that soaring paragraph in which the author pays his final tribute to the vision of the founders—now a reality in the success of Megalapolis-Ceres U. The evidence of success is on every hand: the great sprawling campuses, the seemingly endless construction, the gigantic and stuffed library, the laboratories and their busy research professors loaded down with federal defense grants, deans hurrying to the airport for these foundation appointments in New York, the hordes of well-fed, happy students, the mighty teams, the thousands of alumni, and the astronomical budget.

There is likewise a familiar pattern in the historical treatment of the achievements and failures of land-grant higher education in general. Who, in writing about these colleges, has failed to note what they and their allied experiment stations have done to create the spectacular agricultural revolution whereby an overwhelming, not to say an embarrassing, plenty has become a reality for the first time in man's million or so years? Who has overlooked the process of democratization of higher education, and with it the equalitarianism of subjects and occupations? No one has missed the missionary zeal of these colleges, manifested not only in their mass-student appeal, but also in their pioneering of adult education services. There are also the colleges' development of engineering and technological education, and their allied contributions to teaching method—the field trip, the laboratory, the learning by doing. Not the least of their achievements is the high place they have won for higher education in the heart of the public.

Anyone could add to the list, yet our thinking about the land-grant idea has become so stereotyped that other equally major achievements are usually overlooked. The same is true for failings. It is time we learned the truth about our past and re-examined our present situation in the light of its enlarged perspective. A thorough examination will probably reveal deficiencies and virtues we never thought we possessed, and it could provide insights for our future and defenses against some of our critics. A number of them have, for example, idealized the older education without apparently knowing what a failure it really was, both in content and in quality. They miss the meaning of the land-grant idea or the situation which called it forth. The new education is said to have killed the grand old liberal arts tradition. It was actually the new education, characterized by the technical-cultural synthesis attempted by the land-grant idea, which has established the broad view of liberal education to which we now officially subscribe.

Many accomplishments of the land-grant colleges have not received the emphasis they deserve. First of all, one of the most important tasks undertaken by early public institutions was their sponsorship and supervision of new public high-school systems. Michigan University began grading high schools in 1871, and thereby set an example for such plains state institutions as the Universities of Arizona and North Dakota. The North Dakota high school system was largely the work of the University, which not only established it but largely managed it during its first twenty years. The pioneers of the land-grant idea clearly intended to establish a unified system progressing from Grade 1 through Grade 16, and even through graduate and professional school.

And this was to be education for all. We hear so much now about the need to raise educational standards that we are likely to be apologetic about the process of democratization. Some have even been persuaded that the attempt was a mistake. Indeed, the combination of new subjects with no faculty qualified to teach them, with no suitable textbooks, and with country school graduates as students, did pull down standards. But this theme has been overworked; the caliber of students admitted to the infant land-grant college was not too much below that

of students admitted to the older eastern colleges
in the 1870's and 1880's. And many of the former more than made up in industry and earnest-
ness what they lacked in preparation. One might
even suggest that in the land-grant institutions
American higher education first really became
serious business. Nor were the early faculties on
the last frontier conspicuously inferior to the
average elsewhere. The West attracted a considerable number of able educators, particularly
those interested in reform; these men hoped
that a new land without the strait jacket of tradition would be more receptive to their ideas
than the older colleges were. When Homer Baxter Sprague, Yale graduate and friend of Daniel
Coit Gilman of Johns Hopkins and Andrew D.
White of Cornell, accepted the presidency of
the University of North Dakota in 1887, he
thought of it as "a romantic undertaking in the
'wild and wooly' West."

In retrospect we can see that easy admission
was an essential step, because enough students
had to be found to justify keeping the colleges

open. A bulwark of the old elitism had been the humility of the masses when it came to intellectual matters. To turn, as we are now doing, to the elevation of standards, is to proceed in the proper order. Among other contemporary devices, the honors course seems to be one that combines quality and mass education with benefit to both. In the current drive for quality, the public institutions, owing to their nature and their commitments, will probably avoid the unedifying oneupmanship contests in which the "prestige" private colleges now engage with such vigor. If the process is not halted, the day may not be far off when one of them will achieve the supreme ploy of admitting no students at all because none is good enough for it.

The states of the "last frontier" owe an unmeasured and largely unacknowledged debt to their public colleges for improving their public services and elevating their general cultural level. It was not Franklin D. Roosevelt in 1933, but Robert M. La Follette in 1901 who first formed a brain trust of expert advisers and administrators drawn from the university campus —La Follette's came from the vigorous University of Wisconsin only a few blocks from the state capitol in Madison. The Wisconsin example was probably most eagerly copied in the western states, owing to the fact that their meager intellectual capital was largely concentrated in the colleges they themselves maintained and had a direct claim upon. The role of the western universities in a variety of reform movements deserves more attention than historians have usually given to it. In North Dakota, the Nonpartisan League, an agrarian reform movement formed in 1915 when the University was only thirty-one years old and the Agricultural College twenty-five, was led largely by graduates of these youthful institutions. It is a matter worthy of some reflection that a state as removed as North Dakota from the mainstreams of intellectual life elected only one governor without a college education in nearly sixty years, and only one such United States senator since 1920. In view of the money and effort Americans have

[69]

put into higher education, it should surprise
no one that the brain trust and educated leadership have been the norm in public affairs much
longer than most people realize, and that this
development has been by no means limited to
the national government. Unquestionably the
tone of public debate and the general conduct
of public office have been elevated in the West
in the past two generations.

The improvement of the cultural level in
the West, or in the nation at large, is harder to
measure, but it has occurred nonetheless. Out
of habit we continue to think and speak of
Americans of today as if they were the Americans of Jackson's time. The fact is that the
American of today is again a "new man," and on
his way to becoming the most cosmopolitan man
on the globe. This new man is a product of the
educational revolution. The Wild West has
been tamed at least as much by the public college as by the good women and the fast guns
who usually get most of the credit. It is the professors who are chiefly responsible for the fact

that the society of western Kansas compares favorably in general sophistication, worldliness,
and manners with that of rural France.

Consider the colleges' role in Americanizing
the hosts of immigrants whose arrival in the
West coincided with the development of the
land-grant idea. It took only one generation,
and often none at all, for North Dakota's Nor-
wegian and Icelandic immigrants, peasants who
could never have aspired to more than an apprenticeship at home, to recognize that the state
colleges were the roads to full social acceptance
and to the opportunity that America promised.
The two immigrants who became governors in
North Dakota did so by way of teachers colleges
and the university.

American public colleges have been playing
an increasingly important role in social adjust-
ments abroad. Such institutions as the University of Wyoming and the University of Arizona
have undertaken the supervision of infant institutions in backward countries, and each year
more and more foreign students come to Amer-

ica to study. A dozen Nigerians trained in political science, engineering, or public health are far more subversive of old systems and centuries-old inertia than any number of CIA filibuster-commando enterprises. Early American example and ideology have been sources of revolution since 1776. Our agents today are the foreign students who study with us and, having seen their Utopia in action, return to their own countries armed with the techniques of change.

One more achievement usually overlooked is the role of the land-grant idea in shaping the character of the modern American military services. Without consciously intending to do so, the Morrill Act's requirement that military training be given in the land-grant colleges, which was supplemented by the National Defense Act of 1916, injected a strong civilian and university influence into the officer corps. Its dilution by a steady stream of civilian-trained personnel has been of great importance to us, especially since we have been forced to develop a large standing army and navy. Had not the ROTC officers

[72]

been available, we would have been forced to enlarge our service academies and thereby have risked developing a European-style military caste. So far, at least in the last two wars, the services have been considerably more civilianized than Americans in general have been militarized, and the ROTC has had no small part in this development.

And now what of the other side of the picture —the failures and the deficiencies of land-grant education? The company histories rarely say much about them, and the most recent general history of the land-grant colleges is equally reticent. Even neutral surveys of current practices are likely to end in generalizations that affect no one specifically. A few years ago the State Board of Higher Education of North Dakota invited the United States Office of Education to study the colleges it supervised and to make recommendations. Anyone unfamiliar with the sensitive nature of state colleges might assume that in view of their professed ideals of freedom and truth, the colleges would have welcomed the opportunity to make the case for a rationalized state system of higher education. The contrary was true; neither the institutions' leaders nor a good part of their faculties really wanted an impartial outside appraisal of their operations, and there was undoubtedly more than a little truth to the faculty cynics' gleeful tales of efforts to conceal doubtful procedures, or to inflate such meritorious activities as might be likely to impress the survey team. There was a general sigh of relief when the report turned out to be an innocuous document which criticized no one severely and offered few solutions to the truly serious problem of too many state colleges and too little revenue to support them properly. It is rare indeed when anyone announces nowadays that the institution he represents has ever been guilty of a failure or mistaken policy that could not have been remedied by spending more money. A recently appointed provost at one of our western universities clearly marked himself as a maverick by announcing shortly after he took office that his institution was no better than second-rate, and that a supreme effort was necessary if it were ever to rise above mediocrity. It would have been more conventional for him to claim that his law school was the "best west of the Mississippi," his engineering school "second only to M.I.T.," and so on.

How do we account for this extreme sensitivity to really meaningful criticism? Have educators substituted advertising and salesmanship for the scholarly objectivity their faculties profess in their teaching and research? If so, we have a curious paradox. On the one hand, "Democracy's Colleges" pride themselves on their accomplishments in elevating the level of public information and judgment. On the other, they do not share Jefferson's belief that the general public they serve and profess to respect is capable of knowing the unvarnished truth and of acting wisely on it. The old view of two intellectual worlds, the educated and the uneducated, apparently still survives in the very colleges founded to bring those worlds together.

Mistrust of the masses' intellectual capacity

may be directly related to one of the most significant and disturbing failures of the land-grant idea—the inability of "Democracy's College" to arrive at some satisfactory combination of general education and technical-vocational training. A great step forward was taken when such subjects as modern languages, the sciences, engineering, and agriculture received collegiate status, yet not at the price of abolishing the older cultural curriculum. Professor Edward Danforth Eddy has written that the mixture of practical and cultural education within a single institution is the most significant contribution the land-grant idea has made to American higher education.[1] It should be added that this was of particular importance in the West, because few independent or sectarian liberal arts colleges achieved real influence there.

Yet, the full possibilities of the combination are by no means realized. The public university's liberal arts college has all too often occupied an inferior position.[2] If salaries, prestige, and rate of promotion are any reliable indication, the liberal arts college has the lowest place in the collegiate hierarchy on land-grant campuses, despite all the pious utterances about educating the whole man. It is significant that one of the last of its suborganizations to be recognized by the Association of Land-Grant Colleges and State Universities was that of the liberal arts deans—this occurred after World War II. At its worst, the liberal arts branch is pushed down to the status of a lowly "service" agency, providing technical writing instruction for pre-engineers, constitutional history for lawyers, organic chemistry for the medics, and a winter haven for the aimless. It is a safe guess that faculty morale and respect for one's own profession is lower in the liberal arts college than in the medical school. One can say the same for their students. The job of a liberal arts dean on a state university or land-grant campus is one of the most demanding in the academic world. If he is not the ablest dean on campus, the educational ideal he represents and must articulate is unlikely to receive

[77]

the respect and consideration everyone says it deserves.

Incomplete educational synthesis is not entirely the fault of aggressive professional departments and their appeal to practical-minded legislatures and career-bound students. Part of the difficulty lies in the liberal arts colleges themselves, in their past failures to educate, when they had the chance, the people who now staff the professional schools. Uncertainty within the liberal arts faculties about what is a proper program has been no help. This has not been entirely a failure of intellect; campus vested interests have likewise been responsible. To admit that courses in World Civilization or English Literature are *the* basic courses to be required of every student may mean that the departments which teach these courses are sufficiently swollen to offer "graduate" programs and to become powers in campus politics, while departments without large patronage remain insignificant.

Our failure to do as well as we once hoped in

training citizens—leaders and creative men and women—is related to our incomplete success in achieving an educational synthesis. The old course in moral philosophy taught by the president to the seniors, naive and didactic though it appears to us, may have been on the right track. A half-century ago there was much talk of citizenship training as a function of higher education, but the term has fallen into disrepute, and we rarely use it without slight embarrassment. Gilman, White, Sprague, and others of their kind were convinced that this was as much the responsibility of higher education as intellectual or professional training, and that it could not be achieved without conscious effort. We have not added much to this, except to exhort each other to train leaders. More recently the formula has been enriched by some vague concept of creativity, but how this is developed no one seems to know. An essential in our predecessors' concept of citizenship training was exemplary character in the professor. It is an element now often overlooked when faculty—

[79]

and deans—are chosen. We should have no reason to be surprised when some of our students
do not turn out well after prolonged association
with professors who, however brilliant in a specialized field of knowledge, are ignoble people,
or when students become convinced that life is
some sort of racket after being exposed to the
open cynicism that permeates intercollegiate
athletics.

The increased proportion of college-educated
public officials has made our public services
more efficient and less corrupt than they were
a century ago. A far greater number of young
men and women are graduating from college
than did then, but can we say that we do any
better, or even as well, as the old colleges in improving students' character, or in turning as
large a proportion of those we encounter into
high-minded leaders as our less expertly trained
predecessors seemed somehow to do? A great
many of our graduates never amount to much,
either in the conventional sense of "success" or
as human beings, and far too many of them seem

to lack either sound judgment or any clear sense of their public responsibilities. Something is manifestly wrong, when graduates of our colleges and universities are taken in by the irrationalities and the spiteful irresponsibility of John Birchism. My impression may be wrong, but it seems to me that graduates of the land-grant institutions, Democracy's own colleges, have been more prominent in such movements in recent years than have been the graduates of the rich private institutions.

Much has been said and written about the great service of the land-grant colleges to their respective areas, about their missionary spirit, their concern for the general public, and their practical contributions to the welfare of state and nation. But even here there have been some serious omissions. We can all cite examples of departments in state universities which take no interest in providing graduate training for a region, or ignore their opportunity, or duty, if you will, to provide leadership for departments of neighboring and smaller colleges. I once initiated and helped to organize a state social science association at a time when I held a position at a state university, but it took me twelve years to realize that this was something that needed to be done. In another state I attended a regional social science meeting on the state university campus in a building adjacent to the history office building, but not a single university historian bothered to attend.

A related failing has been academic departments' abdication of any responsibility for what is taught in the public schools. A number of land-grant universities, among them Missouri, Minnesota, and North Dakota, were leaders in the formation of their states' secondary school systems. Not to respect this achievement and the former close, friendly connection between the state colleges and public schools is symptomatic of one of the land-grant universities' most conspicuous failures—their separation, often deliberate, from the lower public schools. With the exception of the professional education departments, college faculties have lost interest almost entirely except to act as critics without anything concrete to suggest, their criticism consisting mainly of complaints about the quality of the students turned out by the high schools. Methods courses for undergraduates preparing to teach are either lost by default or are shunted off on a defenseless young instructor who is himself trying to learn to teach. Summer courses for public school teachers are customarily offered, but the high-school teacher graduate student is often held in half-amused contempt; the loudest faculty critics proudly refuse to teach summer school at all. The teachers have turned from the "subject matter" departments, producing such consequences as an entire social science curriculum for a state prepared without the advice of a single social scientist or historian from the colleges. In short, where once the professors had everything to say about what was taught in the high schools, they now—or until very recently—find themselves with no voice at all. Liberal arts faculties possibly have been the most neglectful of the public service aspect of their work, perhaps because their relation to public service is less obvious than is that of a geologist, for example.

What this comes down to is really part of a larger failing, that of leadership in general. Land-grant institutions on the last frontier have often lacked adventuresomeness, and oddly enough this fault has become more marked as they have become more firmly established. Institutions which once fermented with the ideas of a Homer Baxter Sprague, who was too radical for Connecticut and eventually for North Dakota, have become careful, anxious to please or to look good in the eyes of other administrations and the accrediting agencies. The land-grant idea, influential though it has been in effecting a revolution in all of American higher education, has in turn imposed a conformity of its own. Unlike the private colleges, land-grant institutions have not developed individual personalities indigenous to a geographical location and expressing a peculiar historical development. In our time the launching of a new cur-

[84]

riculum is likely to be preceded by a search of other colleges' catalogs; new course descriptions smell of plagiarism. A recent writer has excused the deficiencies of elementary and secondary education in America by blaming the public, which he says gets what it wants in education.[3] He forgets that public education is something that the public was *taught* to want by vehement and courageous reformers. The first Morrill Act was actually opposed in Congress by representatives from the West. And land-grant colleges did not win general acceptance until legislators, regents, and the public were persuaded to want them. This took vision, performance, and damn-the-consequences courage.

Other educational developments in a century of revolution need closer examination than they often get. There is the partial failure in women's education. Here the land-grant colleges may be the major culprits, because it was they who developed such courses as home economics and the half-professions of medical and dental technician and the like, thereby diverting women from the tougher intellectual and professional programs which the first militantly feminist coeds of the 1880's and 1890's were prepared to move into. We have certainly not utilized the capacities of half our population as thoroughly as have Finland and Russia, for example. In these countries a great many women are practicing medicine, and women dentists outnumber the men. By contrast, in the Great Plains, an area suffering from a shortage of physicians, a smaller proportion of women college graduates in the 1960's is entering the medical profession than entered it a half-century and more ago.

The strengths and weaknesses of the administrative setup in public colleges are seldom dealt with concretely, although there is no lack of studies of administration. Professors who write college histories often organize their work by administrations, but they accept without examination the old aphorism that faculties make the university, presumably independently of the quality of their administrations. The immense relief from detail that an efficient administration can provide for those who teach is rarely taken into account—anyone who has ever taught in a small high school or in a badly run college will understand what I mean. And few academic historians ever seem to recognize that it is the administration and not the faculty which leads the American university. George Schmidt has observed in his history of the liberal arts college that the most important person in the early college *was* the president, implying that this is no longer so.[4] It seems clear that the prestige and vigor of the land-grant colleges, indeed of all colleges, still rise or fall with the capacity of their administrations. Indeed, the presidents' mandate to lead goes beyond heading their institutions; it extends to giving direction and guidance to governing boards, to the state legislatures, and to an entire state. Few private colleges afford so impressive and challenging a constituency to their leaders.

Land-grant colleges are also involved with problems associated with public support and public control. In the centennial year of 1962, as was to be expected, "company" historians paid fulsome tribute to those farsighted men who had laid the foundations of our great public universities. It was the exception when anyone gave equal consideration to the problems raised by public control itself. Yet everyone knows that public institutions are peculiarly subject to irresponsible interference. Time after time, just as we are about to congratulate ourselves that the worst times have passed, new instances of interferences come to our attention. The supposedly free and easy West has been at least as guilty as any other section of abusing its universities. Regents searching for subversion in college textbooks in Wyoming, a vigorous effort to improve academic quality and to protect campus freedom interpreted as evidence of subversive tendencies at the University of Colorado, these and other abuses are too recent and too ominous to allow for complacency. We should remember that few if any church colleges have risen to first-class status without cutting their church connections, that is, freeing themselves from narrow ideological control. This fact has serious implications for the public colleges, and their friends do them no service by dismissing the doubts of honest, public-spirited men about the prospects of increasing federal aid as just another facet of right-wing carping about high taxes. It is only proper to add in this respect, however, that distance from the source of funds does lend a degree of immunity. So far in our educational history there has been less inclination toward ideological interference from Washington than there has been from Bismarck or Boise, from the local chapter of the American Legion or influential local churchmen.

This is a unique time for higher education, and especially for our great public institutions. Not since Horace Mann's fight to establish public schools has there been such public interest in education. There is much criticism, and much is deserved. Some is based on unacceptable aims, half-information, and often the spite and selfishness of those who object to public services of any kind. The only answer to critics and friends

[89]

alike is complete and candid information. This means more than new self-surveys of current operations. Democracy's College is now a century old. Enough time has passed to allow the historian the long look backward which is necessary for a thorough analysis. This must be cast in terms of specifics: names must be named, individual practices described, institutions and men made to bear the blame for their omissions and shortcomings, as well as to accept the praise for their accomplishments. The whole must be firmly related to the entire fabric of American development. It is only from honest, objective assessments, not from generalizations which point no direct accusing finger, that we can hope to find out what ails us and what is really right with us.

The land-grant idea is no longer in danger; it is accepted and respected. There is little doubt that it will become even more influential in its second century than it was at the celebration of its first centennial. Honest appraisal of its past cannot do it any harm and can do great good.

The skeletons that rattle about are more than matched by the records of great men, by countless instances of selfless devotion to the public good, by great ideas and noble ideals, and by the grand accomplishment of the land-grant idea, the transformation of an entire society.

NOTES

1. *Colleges for Our Land and Time* (New York: Harper & Row, 1956), p. 275.

2. A recently published history of the University of Arizona gives less space to the College of Liberal Arts than to any other major branch of the University.

3. Raymond Harris, *American Education: Facts, Fancy, and Folklore* (New York: Random House, 1961).

4. *The Liberal Arts College* (New Brunswick: Rutgers University Press, 1957).

A NOTE ABOUT THE AUTHOR

Louis G. Geiger, Professor of History and Chairman of the Department at Colorado College, was born in Boonville, Missouri, in 1913. He holds degrees from Central Missouri State College (B.S., 1934) and the University of Missouri (M.A., 1940; Ph.D., 1948). In 1954–1955 he was Fulbright Lecturer in American Civilization at the University of Helsinki, and in 1963–1964 Visiting Professor at Jadavpur University, Calcutta. His published works include *Joseph W. Folk of Missouri* (1953) and *University of the Northern Plains* (1958).

Professor Geiger writes the publisher that he "became interested in the history of higher education in the West when writing the history of the University of North Dakota. While working on the book I turned the attention of my graduate seminar in Populism and Progressivism more and more toward attitudes on higher education in regions where organized agrarianism has been strong."